The Edible Pyramid

GOOD EATING EVERY DAY

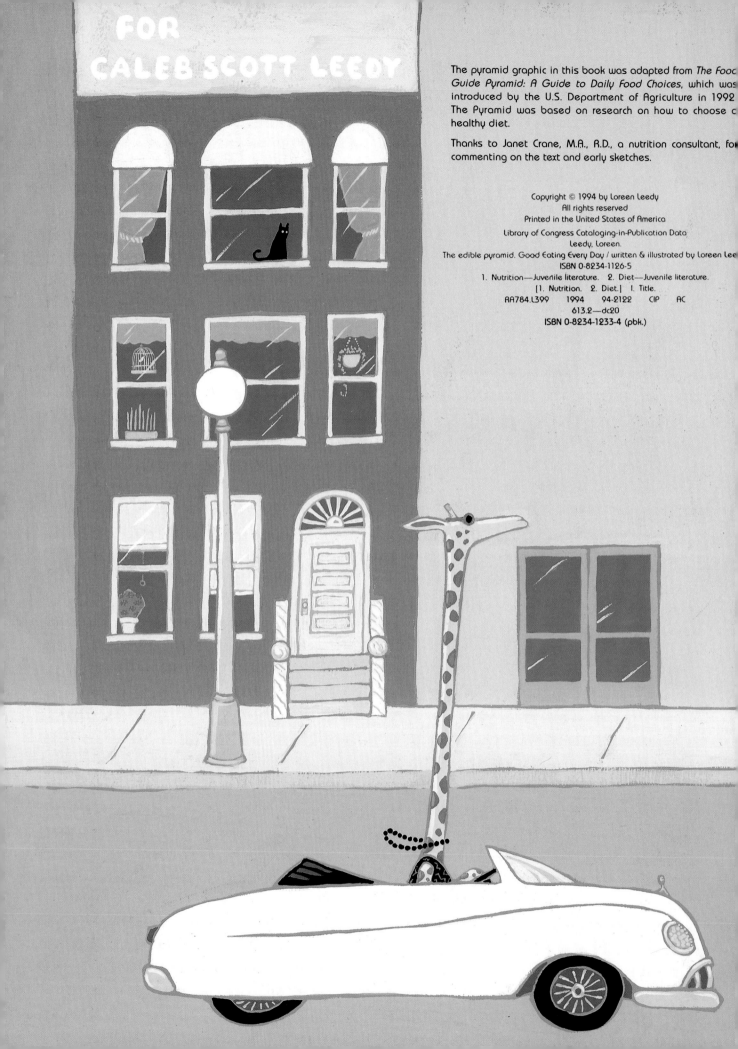

FOR
CALEB SCOTT LEEDY

The pyramid graphic in this book was adapted from *The Food Guide Pyramid: A Guide to Daily Food Choices*, which was introduced by the U.S. Department of Agriculture in 1992. The Pyramid was based on research on how to choose a healthy diet.

Thanks to Janet Crane, M.A., R.D., a nutrition consultant, for commenting on the text and early sketches.

Library of Congress Cataloging-in-Publication Data
Leedy, Loreen.
The edible pyramid. Good Eating Every Day / written & illustrated by Loreen Leedy
ISBN 0-8234-1126-5
1. Nutrition—Juvenile literature. 2. Diet—Juvenile literature.
[1. Nutrition. 2. Diet.] I. Title.
RA784.L399   1994   94-2122   CIP   AC
613.2—dc20
ISBN 0-8234-1233-4 (pbk.)

The Edible Pyramid

GOOD EATING

EVERY DAY

written & illustrated by

Loreen Leedy

Holiday House, New York

On the day of the grand opening of The Edible Pyramid restaurant, customers lined up to get inside.

I hope there is a salad bar.

I hope they have seafood.

Our pyramid menu helps
you plan good meals...
We suggest eating
a variety of foods.
It's healthy to eat
more servings from
the bottom rows
of the pyramid.

Fats
and
Ea

Milk,
Yogurt, and
Cheese group
2-3 servings a day

Vegetable group
3-5 servings a day

Bread, Cereal, Rice, & Pasta group

YOUR DAILY

BREAD, CEREAL, RICE, PASTA

Let's start at the base of the pyramid. Here are the BREADS we make.

whole wheat

corn bread

We use CEREAL and RICE in all sorts of ways.

BREAD, CEREAL, RICE, PASTA ▶

rice

barley soup

granola

corn grits

bran muffin

wild rice

millet

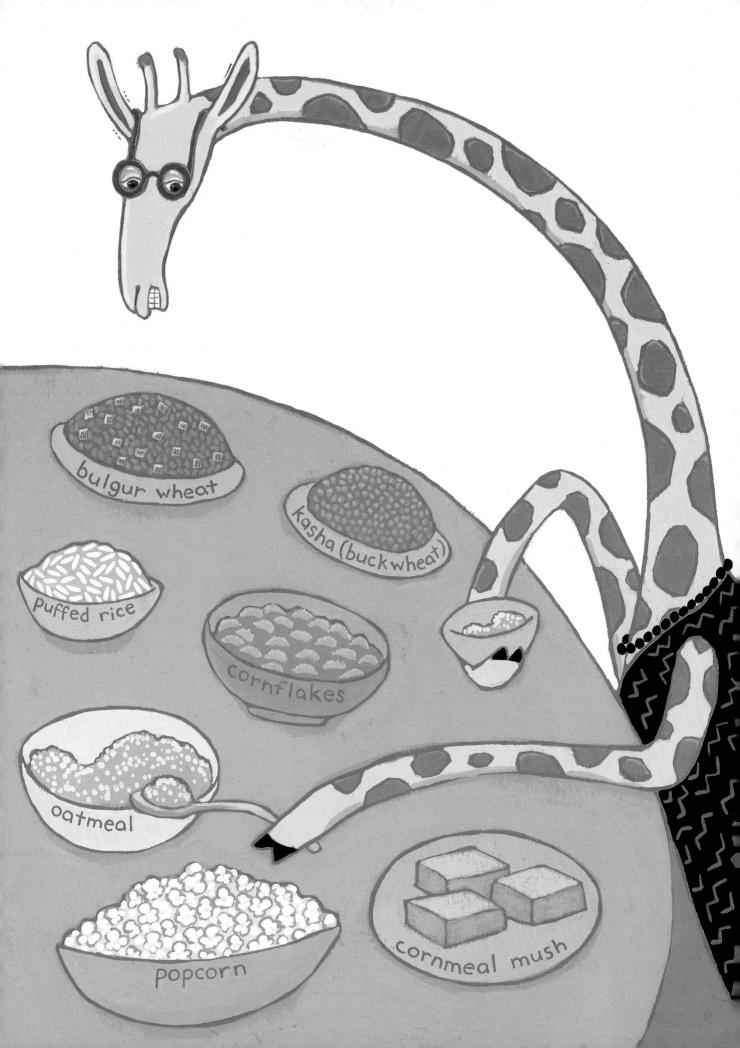

Now we move up a row in the pyramid. **VEGETABLES** come in delicious colors.

FRUIT

FRUIT is naturally sweet.

blueberry

orange

grape

raisin

raspberry

lime

grape juice

kiwi

watermelon

pear

peach

cherry

banana

cantaloupe

apple

lemon

strawberry

▲ MEAT, POULTRY, EGGS, FISH, DRY BEANS, NUTS

Here are just a few
of the ways we serve
MEAT, POULTRY,
FISH, and EGGS.

beefsteak

meatballs

ham

flounder

tuna

caviar
(fish eggs)

shrimp

"POULTRY" means chicken, turkey, and other birds we eat.

chicken soup

chicken

turkey burger

turkey

poached egg

fried egg

Pistachio

almond

Peanut

PEANUT
BUTTER

cashew

pecan

The Nut House

sunflower seed

walnut

Pumpkin seed

hazelnut

Brazil nut

FATS, OILS, SWEETS

FATS, OILS, and SWEETS are at the top. The tip of the pyramid is the smallest part, to remind us to eat only a little.

Just one more...

Salad Dressing

butter

cream

margarine

candy

chocolate

cookies

sugar

honey

The menu says to eat 6 to 11 servings of BREAD, CEREALS, and PASTA a day. Isn't that a lot?

Let's count servings...
2 of bread,
1 of pasta, and
1 of crackers...
equals 4 servings just in this meal!

◄ 1 slice bread

◄ 1 slice bread

◄ $\frac{1}{2}$ cup pasta salad

◄ several crackers

Sometimes, foods are mixed together, like in pizza. Just estimate how many servings of each food group there are.

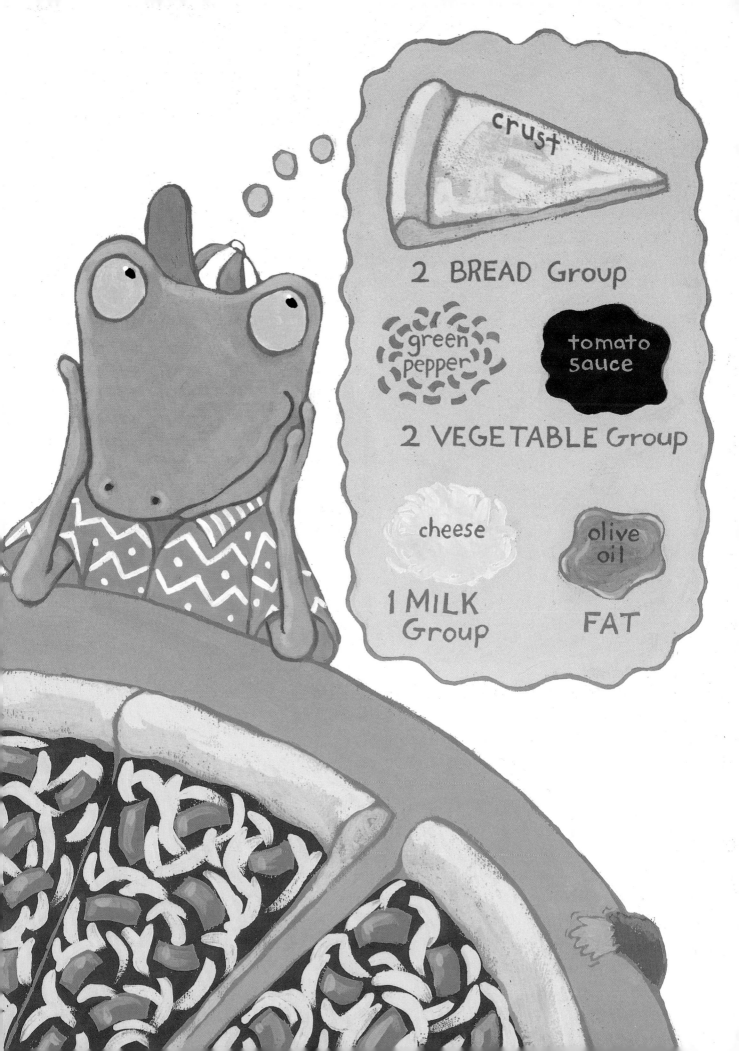

I think everyone has plenty to eat.

Just remember to use the pyramid as a guide to which foods to eat, and how many servings every day!